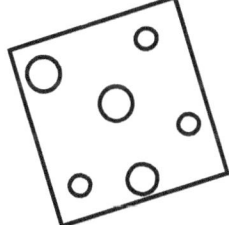
il formaggio

the cheese
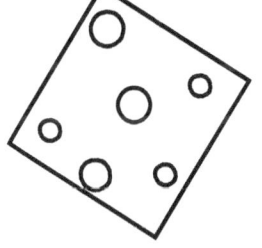

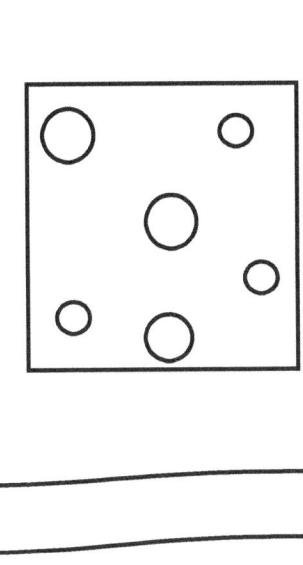

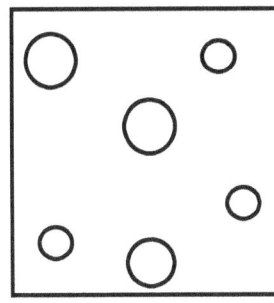

il panino

the sandwich

 **la macchina**

the car

il pullman

the bus

l'aeroplano

the plane

la mucca

the cow

l'insalata

the salad

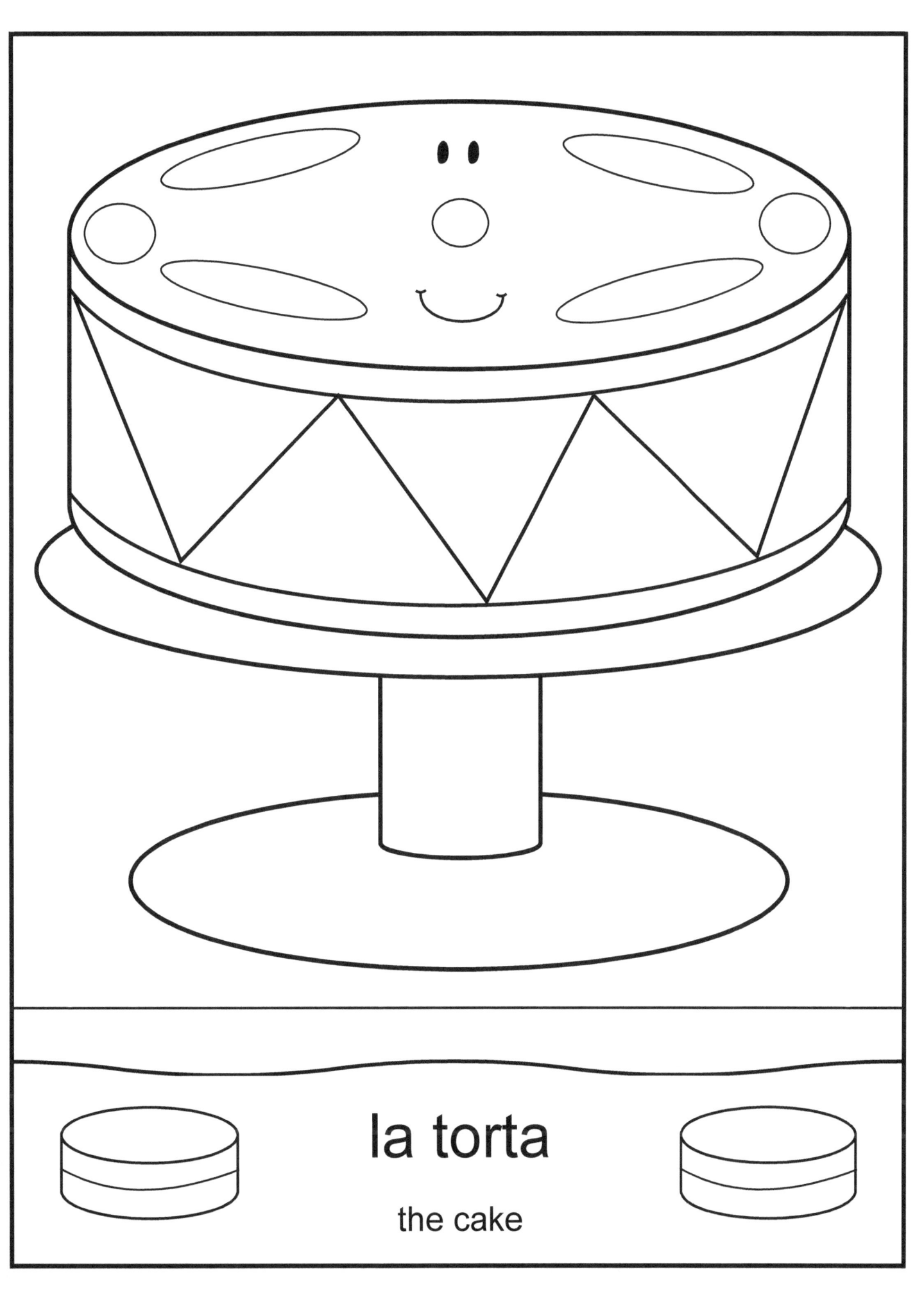

l'elefante

the elephant

il coccodrillo

the crocodile

la rana

the frog

la piscina

the swimming pool

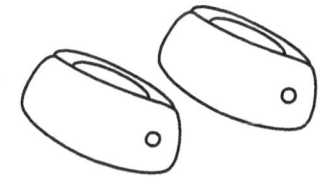

il supermercato

the supermarket

la carota

the carrot

 # i piselli

the peas

I hope you have enjoyed the colouring pages in this book! Try to look back at the Italian words from time to time to help you remember them.

Reviews help other readers discover my books so please consider leaving a short review on the site where the book was purchased. Your feedback is important to me.

Thank you! And have fun learning Italian! It's a lovely language to learn!

Joanne Leyland

For more information about learning Italian and the great books by Joanne Leyland go to **https://funitalianforkids.com**

For information about learning French, Spanish, German, Italian or English as a foreign language go to **https://learnforeignwords.com**

© Copyright Joanne Leyland 2023
No part of this book can be photocopied or reproduced digitally without the prior written agreement of the author.

Young Cool Kids Learn Italian by Joanne Leyland
Fun activities & colouring pages in Italian for 5 - 7 year olds

Ideal for young children learning Italian. This enjoyable book introduces and practises key vocabulary for popular topics.

The fun activities for practising Italian include matching Italian words to pictures by drawing a line, circling the correct word, copying words or writing just a few words per page.

Topics: numbers, the toy shop, greetings, a trip to the beach, zoo animals, the countryside, colours, the birthday party

ISBN: 978-1-914159-00-8

Sophie And The Italian Magician by Joanne Leyland
First Words In Italian - Two Great Stories:
At the Fair / Sophie's Birthday Party

With two great stories in each book, learning Italian is fun with the Italian magician! In the first story, the Italian magician asks everyone to clap and say three times various Italian words as he makes a coin vanish and some animals appear. In the second story, it's Sophie's birthday party and the Italian magician makes teddies of various colours appear, as everyone claps and says three times some colours in Italian.

ISBN: 978-1-914159-13-8

Also available by Joanne Leyland

French
Young Cool Kids Learn French
French Colouring Book For Kids Ages 5 - 7
First Words In French Teacher's Resource Book
Stories for 3-7 year olds: Jack And The French Languasaurus - Books 1, 2 & 3,
Daniel And The French Robot - Books 1, 2 & 3, Sophie And The French Magician
Cool Kids Speak French - Books 1, 2 & 3 *(for kids ages 7 - 11)*
French Word Games - Cool Kids Speak French
Photocopiable Games For Teaching French
40 French Word Searches Cool Kids Speak French
First 100 Words In French Coloring Book Cool Kids Speak French
French at Christmas time
On Holiday In France Cool Kids Speak French
Cool Kids Do Maths In French
Stories in French: Un Alien Sur La Terre, Le Singe Qui Change De Couleur, Tu As Un Animal?

Italian
Young Cool Kids Learn Italian
Italian Colouring Book For Kids Ages 5 - 7
Sophie And The Italian Magician *(a story for 3-7 year olds)*
Cool Kids Speak Italian - Books 1, 2 & 3 *(for kids ages 7 - 11)*
Italian Word Games - Cool Kids Speak Italian
Photocopiable Games For Teaching Italian
40 Italian Word Searches Cool Kids Speak Italian
First 100 Words In Italian Coloring Book Cool Kids Speak Italian
On Holiday In Italy Cool Kids Speak Italian
Stories in Italian: Un Alieno Sulla Terra, La Scimmia Che Cambia Colore, Hai Un Animale Domestico?

German
Young Cool Kids Learn German
German Colouring Book For Kids Ages 5 - 7
Cool Kids Speak German - Books 1, 2 & 3 *(for kids ages 7 - 11)*
German Word Games - Cool Kids Speak German
Photocopiable Games For Teaching German
40 German Word Searches Cool Kids Speak German
First 100 Words In German Coloring Book Cool Kids Speak German

Spanish
Young Cool Kids Learn Spanish
Spanish Colouring Book For Kids Ages 5 - 7
First Words In Spanish Teacher's Resource Book
Stories for ages 3-7: Daniel And The Spanish Robot Books 1,2&3, Sophie And The Spanish Magician
Cool Kids Speak Spanish - Books 1, 2 & 3 *(for kids ages 7 - 11)*
Spanish Word Games - Cool Kids Speak Spanish
Photocopiable Games For Teaching Spanish
40 Spanish Word Searches Cool Kids Speak Spanish
First 100 Words In Spanish Coloring Book Cool Kids Speak Spanish
Spanish at Christmas time
On Holiday In Spain Cool Kids Speak Spanish
Cool Kids Do Maths In Spanish
Stories: Un Extraterrestre En La Tierra, El Mono Que Cambia De Color, Seis Mascotas Maravillosas

English as a second language / foreign language
English For Kids Ages 5 - 7
English Colouring Book For Children Ages 3 - 7
Cool Kids Speak English - Books 1, 2 & 3 *(for kids ages 7 - 11)*
First Words In English 100 Words To Colour & Learn
Fun Word Search Puzzles

www.ingramcontent.com/pod-product-compliance
Lightning Source LLC
Chambersburg PA
CBHW081727100526
44591CB00016B/2528

Also available by Joanne Leyland

French
Young Cool Kids Learn French
French Colouring Book For Kids Ages 5 - 7
First Words In French Teacher's Resource Book
Stories for 3-7 year olds: Jack And The French Languasaurus - Books 1, 2 & 3,
Daniel And The French Robot - Books 1, 2 & 3, Sophie And The French Magician
Cool Kids Speak French - Books 1, 2 & 3 *(for kids ages 7 - 11)*
French Word Games - Cool Kids Speak French
Photocopiable Games For Teaching French
40 French Word Searches Cool Kids Speak French
First 100 Words In French Coloring Book Cool Kids Speak French
French at Christmas time
On Holiday In France Cool Kids Speak French
Cool Kids Do Maths In French
Stories in French: Un Alien Sur La Terre, Le Singe Qui Change De Couleur, Tu As Un Animal?

Italian
Young Cool Kids Learn Italian
Italian Colouring Book For Kids Ages 5 - 7
Sophie And The Italian Magician *(a story for 3-7 year olds)*
Cool Kids Speak Italian - Books 1, 2 & 3 *(for kids ages 7 - 11)*
Italian Word Games - Cool Kids Speak Italian
Photocopiable Games For Teaching Italian
40 Italian Word Searches Cool Kids Speak Italian
First 100 Words In Italian Coloring Book Cool Kids Speak Italian
On Holiday In Italy Cool Kids Speak Italian
Stories in Italian: Un Alieno Sulla Terra, La Scimmia Che Cambia Colore, Hai Un Animale Domestico?

German
Young Cool Kids Learn German
German Colouring Book For Kids Ages 5 - 7
Cool Kids Speak German - Books 1, 2 & 3 *(for kids ages 7 - 11)*
German Word Games - Cool Kids Speak German
Photocopiable Games For Teaching German
40 German Word Searches Cool Kids Speak German
First 100 Words In German Coloring Book Cool Kids Speak German

Spanish
Young Cool Kids Learn Spanish
Spanish Colouring Book For Kids Ages 5 - 7
First Words In Spanish Teacher's Resource Book
Stories for ages 3-7: Daniel And The Spanish Robot Books 1,2&3, Sophie And The Spanish Magician
Cool Kids Speak Spanish - Books 1, 2 & 3 *(for kids ages 7 - 11)*
Spanish Word Games - Cool Kids Speak Spanish
Photocopiable Games For Teaching Spanish
40 Spanish Word Searches Cool Kids Speak Spanish
First 100 Words In Spanish Coloring Book Cool Kids Speak Spanish
Spanish at Christmas time
On Holiday In Spain Cool Kids Speak Spanish
Cool Kids Do Maths In Spanish
Stories: Un Extraterrestre En La Tierra, El Mono Que Cambia De Color, Seis Mascotas Maravillosas

English as a second language / foreign language
English For Kids Ages 5 - 7
English Colouring Book For Children Ages 3 - 7
Cool Kids Speak English - Books 1, 2 & 3 *(for kids ages 7 - 11)*
First Words In English 100 Words To Colour & Learn
Fun Word Search Puzzles

www.ingramcontent.com/pod-product-compliance
Lightning Source LLC
Chambersburg PA
CBHW081727100526
44591CB00016B/2528